D1279144

TOTALLY GROSS HISTORY™

THE TOTALLY GROSS HISTORY OF
ANCIENT CHINA

JENNIFER CULP

rosen publishing's
rosen
central

Published in 2016 by The Rosen Publishing Group, Inc.
29 East 21st Street, New York, NY 10010

Copyright © 2016 by The Rosen Publishing Group, Inc.

First Edition

Library of Congress Cataloging-in-Publication Data
Culp, Jennifer.
The totally gross history of ancient China/Jennifer Culp.—First edition.
        pages cm.—(Totally gross history)
Bugs, Birds' Nests, and Bears' Paws—Pigs, Poop, and (Toilet) Paper—Beauty and Pain—
Cruelty and Capital Punishment.
Includes bibliographical references and index.
Audience: Grade level 5–8.
ISBN 978-1-4994-3758-4 (library bound) — ISBN 978-1-4994-3756-0 (pbk.) —
ISBN 978-1-4994-3757-7 (6-pack)
1. China—Civilization—Juvenile literature. I. Title.
DS721.C97 2016
931—dc23

                                                                        2015034072

Manufactured in the United States of America

CONTENTS

INTRODUCTION

The People's Republic of China is the most populous country in the world. More than a billion citizens live within its borders, which contain nearly 4 million square miles (10 million square kilometers) of land across the continent of Asia. China also boasts one of the world's oldest and most diverse civilizations, stretching back thousands of years before the beginning of the Common Era. To put the length of China's history into perspective, think about it this way: we are currently a little over two thousand years into the Common Era. China's history spans that length of time, plus many thousands of years before that. Archaeologists have even found evidence of domestication of animals, production of silk, and early systems of Chinese writing before the beginning of recorded history, back into prehistoric times.

For most of its existence, China was ruled by hereditary dynasties—families who passed along the title of emperor and the mandate to rule. When a particular dynasty lost the Mandate of Heaven (i.e., stopped doing a good job of ruling and got overthrown by someone else), a new dynasty would replace it. Rule transferred between many groups over the course of China's history as different warlords and various ethnic groups rose to power, only to eventually fall and be replaced by another dynasty. The last dynastic group to rule, the Qing dynasty, ended in 1912, and the country became the Communist-ruled People's Republic of China in 1949.

The Great Wall of China was constructed over thousands of years and spans more than 13,000 miles. China was among the earliest, largest, and most advanced world civilizations.

Chinese people invented silk, gunpowder, paper, and reproducible printing with ink and carved wooden blocks. The philosophies of Confucianism and Taoism rose from China, and its people developed the practice of Zen Buddhism after the religion of Buddhism entered the country via India. China has long been home to astronomers and mathematicians, and developed an advanced (and effective) system of medicine long before the rise of Western pharmacy. Monuments to Chinese ingenuity and enterprise still stand in the form of the more than 12,427-mile (20,000-km) Great Wall of China and the terracotta army of soldiers that stand guard over the mausoleum of the First Qin Emperor.

The Chinese civilization is very old and has a rich and diverse history... and, as with every civilization, some of it is pretty gross.

CHAPTER ONE

BUGS, BIRDS' NESTS, AND BEARS' PAWS

Tastes differ from place to place, time to time, and person to person. Food that tastes delicious to one person might be disgusting to another, and most people aren't overly fond of unfamiliar foods from other countries on first bite. That's totally normal! Some of the things ancient Chinese people ate, however, stand out as particularly gross by contemporary Western standards.

DELICIOUS DOG

Beef is a common dietary staple of many modern North Americans, but it wasn't often eaten throughout the history of China. For one thing, cattle were valuable draught animals, used to pull carts and farming equipment. Additionally, the consumption of beef became even more unpopular as Buddhism spread through China at the start of the Common Era because many of the religion's sects frown on beef consumption. "Oxen were regarded as members of the family, and they and cows were ordinarily kept by farmers for as long as possible. People condemned the

This golden statue of a horned cow in a Buddhist temple in Kunming, Younnan, underscores the sacred status of cattle in ancient China. The diets of cultures can change a great deal over the centuries.

slaughter of oxen, looked down on butchers, and were sad when finally they did sell an ox or cow," writes Frederick Simoons in the book *Food in China*. So what kind of animals did people in long-ago China eat? Well, for one: dogs.

A LONG TRADITION

Dogs, along with pigs, were one of the most important domestic animals kept by farmers in China as far back as 6500 BCE.

Early Chinese written records show that dogs were not only used for hunting and guarding, but were also a major source of meat. Dog meat was eaten by commoners and kings. But before they were eaten, what did the dogs eat? Because of their efficient digestive systems, dogs were often left to scavenge on or were deliberately fed human excrement—that is, poop. In the sixteenth century, traveler Gaspar de Cruz wrote of a "thriving" market for dog flesh in Canton and noted that on menus meat from black animals was singled out as being especially nutritious.

The most common preference for dog meat in China was that of suckling pups and puppy hams, according to Simoons, and some Chinese cooks claimed that pork hams could not be cured properly unless there was a dog leg included among them. In other cases, rendered dog fat would be used in food preparation to give certain Chinese dishes a special taste. Dog flesh was particularly popular in the province of Guangdong, apparently, giving rise to a folk saying: "Loaves of steamed bread are afraid of dogs; dogs are afraid of people from Guangdong."

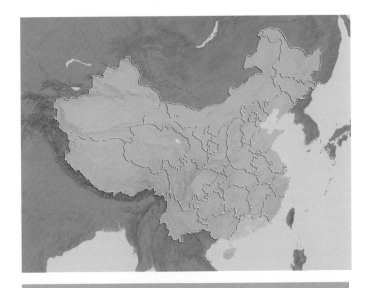

Since 2005, the southeastern province of Guangdong has been the most populous one in the People's Republic of China.

Dog meat wasn't popular throughout all of China at all times, however, and has declined in acceptability since ancient times according to Simoons. A traveler who toured half of China's provinces in the 1800s wrote that dog meat was still consumed by poor people in all of the areas he visited, but very rarely by well-to-do citizens, who ate it only rarely to "stimulate the digestive system."

RATS, SNAKES, AND BUGS

At various times in ancient China, people also ate other unappetizing animals for various reasons. One account of premodern Chinese diets claimed that the Tang people of southern China had a custom of eating live baby rats filled with honey, but if this is true, it does not seem to have been a widespread practice. Most accounts of rat eating in premodern China were focused on medicinal, rather than strictly culinary, purposes. Balding women were known to eat rats, according to Simoons's research, because rat flesh was thought to be effective at restoring hair growth.

Pigeon flesh was considered beneficial for pregnant women and new mothers, and the excrement of white pigeons was used as an antiparasite and antiscurvy medication. Cat skulls, brains, eyes, saliva, and body waste were used to treat rat bites and rat-borne illnesses, though cat meat was rarely eaten at any time in China's history.

Venomous snakes, on the other hand, were eaten as a medicine and a culinary delicacy. "A drink made of snake bile and gall bladder soaked in 'wine' is believed not only to stimulate

Snakes, toads, and lizards are shown here for sale in a market. For the Chinese, consuming certain animals is thought to increase health and well-being. Even nowadays, some Chinese cuisine may seem unusual to outsiders.

health and vigor, but to cure rheumatism," Simoons recounted. Powders made of dried snakeskin were also sold as remedies in Chinese pharmacies.

Insects were commonly consumed as both medicine and food in China, going back thousands of years. The *Compendium of Materia Medica* written by Li Shizhen during the Ming dynasty lists 107 insects and insect products to be used for various medical purposes, and in some parts of the country silkworm pupae were consumed as a food after the silk they created had been processed. Pupae from baked cocoons were preferred to pickled cocoons, according to Simoons's account, and the

FUNGUS CATERPILLAR TEA

Perhaps the grossest insect concoction consumed as a medication and delicacy, as described by researcher W. E. Hoffmann, was caterpillars that contracted a particular fungal infection of the genus *Cordyceps*. The fungus would take root in the caterpillar's neck and grow upward to a height of about 6 to 8 inches (15–20 centimeters) while also burrowing into the creature's body and replacing the tissue in its skin, before killing the caterpillar and dying itself. The fungus-caterpillar corpses would then be prepared in a broth for drinking.

pupae would be fried with onions and sauce or eaten in an omelet with eggs.

OTHER UNUSUAL DELICACIES

"Fish is what I like, so are bear's paws; but if I cannot have both, I will forgo the fish and choose the bear's paws," said Confucian philosopher Mencius, who lived about three hundred years before the Common Era. Like shark's fins, bear's paws were served as a special dish at feasts. Bear's paw was a beloved delicacy in ancient China, as evidenced by the writings of Mencius and others, but became increasingly hard to come by over the years as expansion and industrialization thinned the country's black bear population.

Dishes like this one—sea cucumber in sauce with a side of rice—were once considered exotic by Westerners but have gained much acceptance in recent decades.

Another great delicacy was bêche-de-mer, a dish that Chinese people have been eating for at least one thousand years. This dried product was made from sea cucumbers, unassuming saltwater creatures that quite literally spit their own guts out in order to deter predators. Nineteenth-century writer P. L. Simmonds recounted an English person's impression of the dish:

"dirty light or dark brown in color, stiff and loathsome, and possessed of a strong fishy smell."

And one distinctive delicacy wasn't actually made from an animal at all, but rather *by* it: a translucent, gelatinous nest made by a species of birds called swiftlets. The nests—which hunters would risk life and limb and climb heights of two hundred and 300 feet (60–90 meters) to obtain—were created entirely of "nest cement," a salivary excretion, with a few feathers and bits of greenery stuck in for good measure. These nests are still eaten in modern times, reportedly selling at prices from $375 to $1,000 a pound in Hong Kong in the late 1980s.

Yum! Who's ready for some Chinese food?

CHAPTER TWO

PIGS, POOP, AND (TOILET) PAPER:
POTTY TRAINING AND PROPER HYGIENE

The ancient Chinese were an incredibly clean people. As researcher E. P. Hoyt recounted, "The Chinese practiced personal cleanliness to a remarkable degree. Half a millennium before the birth of Christ, the etiquette of a gentleman demanded that he wash his hands five times a day, take a bath every fifth day and wash his hair every third day." Upper-class Chinese also used detergents to wash their clothes and brushed their teeth with what Hoyt describes as "tooth powder." Compared to Europeans who were their contemporaries, these Chinese gentlemen probably smelled heavenly! But daily life wasn't quite so clean for Chinese peasants. Far from washing their hands five times a day and bathing every weekend, poor farmers who lived in rural areas of China might go their entire lives without ever experiencing a bath as we understand it today.

NATURAL FERTILIZER

It was common to fertilize fields with human feces. The farmers didn't necessarily defecate directly on their fields for fertilization purposes, however. About one hundred years after the start of the Common Era, during the time of the Han dynasty,

This small funerary sculpture of an ancient Chinese pigsty shows the way a pig pen was laid out with stairs and a raised area for dropping food and excrement inside for the pigs' nourishment.

villagers were using outhouses. This arrangement also made feeding livestock more convenient. Basically, the outhouse was set up on top of a platform reached by climbing up a set of stairs. When someone used the toilet in the outhouse, the results fell through a hole in the floor to land in a cesspool near the pigpen…where it became a tasty snack for the pigs. Like dogs, pigs have efficient digestive systems that can actually obtain nutrition from human waste.

Without a sanitary plumbing system in place, ancient Chinese people needed some way to clean up their messes, and both pigs and dogs stepped in to solve the problem. So, the poop got cleaned up and the pigs got fed at the same time! This system wasn't flawless. Human waste contains a *lot* of nasty bacteria, and feeding it to farm animals and spreading it on fields could also spread diseases such as dysentery. The poop-eating pigs and dogs could also cause other problems, as we'll see.

KAIDANGKU AND EARLY POTTY TRAINING

Children of long-ago China didn't wear diapers. Instead they wore a garment called *kaidangku*, basically a pair of pants with no middle seam that left the bottom (and more sensitive parts) open to the air. Kaidangku allowed kids to pee or poop without taking their pants off, bypassing the need for changing diapers entirely. These open-crotch pants also offered other benefits besides the avoidance of smelly diapers. Rather than waiting until a child was a toddler to start toilet training, rural Chinese parents would start the initial stages earlier. The kaidangku allowed little kids who realized they needed to go to squat

Kaidangku are designed to keep small children's private parts bare so they can learn to relieve themselves without the inconvenience of changing diapers.

and do their business immediately, rather than wait (or possibly fail to wait) for a parent to help them out of their clothes. Kaidangku are still in use throughout China, though even many parents using them at home do use diapers out in public, especially in more populous areas.

This system resulted in babies who were potty trained much more quickly than modern Western toddlers but could occasionally lead to tragedy. Chinese Canadian journalist Jan Wong mentioned one such horror story in her 2011 memoir, writing about a twenty-five-year-old man who sought an operation to replace his missing penis. As a three-month-old peasant child in central China, the man had met with a terrible accident. "In the village, children just squat down wherever they are," the reconstructive surgeon explained to Wong. "There are always lots of dogs and pigs, and they fight to eat the feces. Sometimes in the commotion, they end up biting off the penis."

Fortunately for this man, he was born at a time when medical science and technology could offer a solution to his problem. A child who suffered the same fate one thousand years ago wouldn't have been so lucky and perhaps could have even died from complications following the injury. Kaidangku are still in use in China today, as Wong's memoir attests, though some modern parents prefer Western-style disposable diapers or even use both—kaidangku at home, diapers when out and about.

BATHROOMS THROUGH THE AGES

As in so many places through the ages, life was more luxurious in ancient China for the rich. Around 500 BCE, wealthy Chinese

THE INVENTION OF TOILET PAPER

Perhaps it should come as no surprise that the Chinese, who invented paper during the time of the Han dynasty in 100 BCE, were the first people to use toilet paper. Yan Zhitui, a scholar and government official of the sixth century CE, wrote a great deal about education and art. He was also the first person in the entire world to make recorded mention of using toilet paper. As Qizhi Zhang writes in the book *An Introduction to Chinese History and Culture*, however, Yan "was anxious to point out that those who adopted this practice should avoid paper which featured any writings from the classics or sages." In fact, his exact words were, "Paper on which there are quotations or commentaries from the Five Classics or the names of sages, I dare not use for toilet purposes."

Ancient Chinese people also invented silk production and silk weaving, activities depicted in this drawing.

people who lived in cities began to have private latrines installed in their homes. These toilets were simple—basically just a hole in the ground with some bricks to squat on—but they were a big improvement over using chamber pots or having to squat out in the street.

During the Tang dynasty (about 700 CE), enterprising businessmen began to build public toilets that could be used for a price. Then they turned around and made further profit by selling the waste collected from these portable restrooms to farmers, who bought the poop to spread it on their fields. According to *History for Kids*, "Businesses made a lot of money selling poop." Convenient toilets didn't become free to the public until around 1000 CE, when the Sung dynasty decided that access to free restrooms would keep the city cleaner. They continued to sell the public's poop as fertilizer for crops, though.

CHAPTER THREE

BEAUTY AND PAIN

Cosmetics have been used by women in China for thousands of years to alter their appearances to suit the beauty standard of the day. Just as in modern times, the processes undertaken in the quest to look beautiful can be, well, pretty gross.

FACE PAINT AND FISH GUTS

"Ancient Chinese makeup was elaborate, daring and by today's standards sometimes alarming," reporter Zhang Lei wrote in a 2012 article for *China Daily*. A popular look from the time of the Tang dynasty called for huge bushy eyebrows, heavily painted lips, and what Zhang describes as "an expansive coating of rouge covering both cheeks." Complete with a bouffant hairstyle, this look might not seem out of place in a contemporary fashion magazine ... but the materials used to make cosmetic products were very different from the safety-regulated makeup we use today.

In order to achieve the thick, wide-browed look of the Tang dynasty, women scraped off their own natural eyebrows and used a dark blue-green pigment

Young women from the Shaanxi province in east central China perform a traditional dance style originated during the Tang dynasty. Modern Chinese are proud to actively preserve ancient arts and culture.

called *dai* to draw on more fashionably shaped brows. At one point, Emperor Xuanzong of the Tang dynasty, who lived in the late seventh to mid-eighth century CE, put out a list of ten fashionable eyebrow styles for the public to follow, including "mandarin duck, five mountains, willow, cloud, hanging leaf, and butterfly." It's a little hard to imagine what his vision for eyebrows shaped like mandarin ducks might have looked like in practice, but it would likely appear strange to modern eyes.

"DRAGONFLY WINGS, BIRD FEATHERS, AND FISH SCALES"

Ancient Chinese lipstick was actually pretty similar to what we use today, if less animal friendly than many of today's cruelty-free brands. Red lip gloss was made from vermilion—the common term for the mineral cinnabar when it's been ground up—and animal grease. The Chinese had been using cinnabar as a red pigment for around 5,500 years by Emperor Xuanzong's time and had actually discovered how to make a synthetic vermilion before the beginning of the Common Era.

The red mineral cinnabar, mined for centuries in China and elsewhere, looks rough in its natural state before it has been carved and polished.

Their way to achieve a bright red dye was actually way less gross than that of their contemporary Europeans, who ground up tiny insects called *Kermes vermilio* in order to achieve the same color.

But Europe didn't have the market cornered on bugs in beauty products. Materials used in Chinese makeup included "dragonfly wings, bird feathers, and fish scales," according to Zhang. Fashionable Chinese ladies of the Tang dynasty also liked to glue decorations to their faces as well, particularly plum flowers and metal and gem flakes. Faux dimples created by gluing shiny black paper on the cheeks were popular during the Song dynasty.

While the thought of sticking gold, silver, and jade flakes to the face doesn't sound so bad, the special glue used to stick them on sounds much less appealing: it was made from fish guts. Still, the smell of dead fish wasn't enough to scare away an ardent lover, nor was the threat of the fish-glue flakes falling off in the middle of a romantic moment. Tang poet Lu Zhaolin wrote wistfully (and somewhat disgustingly) of a beautiful woman's shed face flakes: "She is nowhere to be found, only her smile flakes left behind, like the trace of cicada's slough."

NAILS AND NAIL POLISH

Long-ago Chinese interest in ornament also led to the invention of one of today's most popular beauty products: nail polish. The Chinese started painting their nails three thousand years before the Common Era. That's around the same time that construction of Stonehenge began in England, almost four thousand years before European people made contact with the Americas!

Using a mixture made from materials such as egg whites, gelatin, beeswax, flower and vegetable dyes, and gum arabic, Chinese women who wanted to wear colorful nails painted their fingernails with the mixture and left it on for hours and hours to dry.

During the Zhou dynasty, from the eleventh to third centuries before the Common Era, "women of different classes wore nail polish, whether they were privileged or not," writes Naomi Millburn of Demand Media. During different periods, however, certain colors were reserved for royalty. Around 600 BCE, according to *Origin of Everyday Things*, royals preferred silver and gold polish. Lower-class women were limited to pale pink polish on pain of the death penalty. Later, during the Ming dynasty, the preferred royal polish colors switched to red and black.

During the last imperial dynasty of China, the Qing dynasty, long fingernails—*very* long fingernails—became a status symbol, showing off the wearer's class and status.

As Valerie Garrett explains in the book *Chinese Dress: From the Qing Dynasty to the Present*, "Most people of gentility cultivated at least one long fingernail to show that they did not engage in manual work." Women, but not men, wore special nail guards to protect the prize fingernail (or nails!), made of fine materials like gold, silver, tortoiseshell, or enameled metal, with elaborate designs of lucky symbols. "Often," Garrett wrote, "two different pairs were worn on the third and fourth fingers of each hand." The nail guards also helped improve the appearance of the nails, which grew thick and scaly in texture as they grew in length. Portraits of Manchurian Empress Dowager Cixi, who died in 1908 at the age of seventy-three, show the ruler wearing 6-inch-long (15 cm) gold nail protectors on her ring and pinkie fingers. They "could certainly help her make a point; they're claw-like and scary," wrote NPR's Susan Stamberg.

These cosmetic customs—growing extralong fingernails, gluing metal flakes to the face with fish guts—are pretty gross but really not that much weirder than many current beauty practices (such as wearing acrylic nails or false eyelashes). One long-standing aesthetic custom throughout the history of China stands out as particularly gruesome, however: foot binding.

GOLDEN LOTUS, BROKEN BONES

The origins of the practice of foot binding are debated. According to Marie-Josèphe Bossan's *The Art of the Shoe*,

This oil painting of the Empress Dowager Cixi show the dagger-like fingernail guards the ruler wore on her fourth and fifth fingers.

one Chinese historian claimed that foot binding began with the Empress Ta Ki about a thousand years before the Common Era. According to this story, Empress Ta Ki suffered from clubfoot (a condition in which an infant is born with a severely twisted foot, so the bottom of the foot faces sideways or even up). Wishing to set a standard of beauty and elegance based on her own appearance, Ta Ki ordered the binding of girls' feet so they would resemble her own. Other legends credit the practice to the renowned small-footed beauty of courtesans such as Pan Fei and Yao Niang, who were both remembered fawningly for their graceful dancing. Whatever the custom's actual origin, foot binding became popular during the Song dynasty, and early references to the practice appear in texts from the late eleventh century. Foot binding was widely practiced by the thirteenth century, when European visitors took note of the unfamiliar appearance of bound feet. "Young women always walk so docilely that one foot follows the other by no more than a half-finger length," wrote Marco Polo in his memoirs. The reason for this perceived "grace" was simple: women with bound feet couldn't balance or walk normally and had to do so with tiny, tottering steps.

TORMENT AT A YOUNG AGE

In order to obtain an ideal bound foot shape, binding had to begin before the arch of the foot had a chance to develop. At about the age when kids start kindergarten today, a young Han Chinese girl of the thirteenth century would be forced to begin the process of foot binding. The whole horrible process is described in detail in Beverly Jackson's book *Splendid Slippers* and Howard

S. Levy's book *The Lotus Lovers*. First the feet were soaked in a warm mixture of water, herbs, and animal blood to make them soft, then the toenails were cut back as far as possible.

At this point, the real torture started. To make the feet significantly smaller, the four small toes on each foot were curled under one by one, then squeezed downward into the sole of the foot until they broke. Next, keeping the broken toes held tightly to the sole of the foot, the binder would stretch out the foot and forcibly break the arch of the little girl's foot, crushing the ball of the foot toward the heel. Bandages, which were prepared by

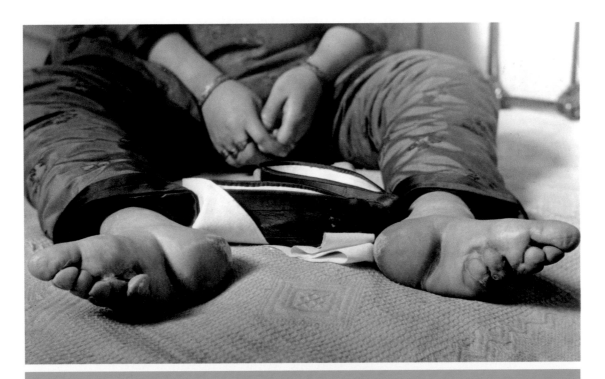

A photograph of a woman's uncovered bound feet, taken around 1949, show the extreme bone deformity caused by the ancient practice of foot binding.

soaking in the same herb and blood solution in which the child's feet were bathed, were then wound tightly around each foot in a figure-eight pattern to squash the broken foot into as small a shape as possible. Then, the binding cloth was sewn together so the girl could not remove or loosen it.

AN ENDLESS PROCESS

After the bone breaking and binding, the torment wasn't over yet. It took a long time for bound feet to "heal" properly, and they required a great deal of maintenance to ensure that infection didn't set in. The mangled feet were regularly unbound so they could be inspected and washed and the nails could be trimmed. The feet were kneaded before rebinding in order to keep the bones soft, and sometimes the soles of the feet would be beaten in order to make the joints and broken bones more pliable. Before rebinding, the feet were soaked so necrotic flesh—that is, *dead flesh*—would fall off. In cases in which it didn't fall off, it would be cut off. Then the feet were rewrapped even more tightly than before.

A DAILY "TREATMENT"

A little girl from a wealthy family would undergo this treatment daily. It was generally undertaken by a professional foot binder or female family member other than the child's mother. As *Splendid Slippers* points out, the mother was typically excluded from the process for fear that she would sympathize with her daughter's pain and fail to keep the bindings tight enough. As the process continued, the girl would be forced to walk long distances on her broken, bound feet in order to break the arches further and allow for tighter binding.

Finally, after about two years of this torture, the feet were numb and the process complete, "creating a deep cleft that could hold a coin in place" instead of the arch of an unbound foot, according to Amanda Foreman, writing for *Smithsonian* magazine. "Once a foot had been crushed and bound," Foreman went on to note, "the shape could not be reversed without a woman undergoing the same pain all over again." And that's assuming it worked properly in the first place—infection could enter the bones and cause the toes to fall off (which was considered a benefit, as it made the foot even smaller), or even cause disease and septic shock that killed the child.

So why did people do it? And why for so long? Hundreds of years ago during the Song dynasty, when the practice was first popularized, writer Che Ruoshui criticized foot binding, stating, "Little children not yet four or five *sui* [i.e. five to seven years old], who have done nothing wrong, nevertheless are made to suffer unlimited pain to bind [their feet] small. I do not know what use this is." Nevertheless, the practice persisted until the twentieth century. For one, it was considered attractive and was an indicator of class, allowing a woman to make an advantageous marriage that would be impossible had her feet remained unbound.

Furthermore, foot binding likely persisted for nearly a millennium because it was so closely associated with the Han Chinese ethnic group, who remained strongly attached to a symbol that united them and set them apart from

DEBAR: A TOAST TO THE GOLDEN LOTUS

Bound feet, with their curled-under toes and crushed arches, were not very pretty outside of their special tiny shoes. Nevertheless, during the time of the Yuan dynasty it became popular to drink from the tiny shoes at celebratory feasts. Marie-Josèphe Bossan, author of *The Art of the Shoe*, attributes this custom to a wealthy, dissolute man named Yang Tieai, who held elaborate banquets where he had guests drink from the tiny shoes worn by women attending the party. "The practice was called 'toasts to the golden lotus,' by its author and it had enthusiasts until the end of the 19th century," Bossan wrote. "This is why lotus lovers consider Yang Tieai the patron saint of the brotherhood of drinkers from the little shoe."

other Chinese peoples. Bound feet were an obvious sign that a woman was Han Chinese, and they resisted mightily when the Manchus rose to power and attempted to outlaw the practice. Additionally, though the custom of foot binding is obviously sexist, it was not merely a situation of atrocity forced on unwilling women by men.

As explained in the book *China Chic: East Meets West*, many Chinese women felt proud of their bound feet and considered themselves to be doing their daughters a great service by binding their feet in turn. According to Professor Dorothy Ko, these beliefs help to explain the longevity of the custom. Foot binding is no longer practiced in modern-day China, but some very old women who had their feet bound as children in the early twentieth century still survive today.

CHAPTER FOUR

CRUELTY AND CAPITAL PUNISHMENT

O f all the disgusting things human beings can do, hurting and killing each other is at the very top of the list. Long-ago Chinese governments sought to punish criminals and deter future crimes, however, and they were horribly inventive in the tortures and executions they doled out to citizens who broke their laws.

CRUEL SANCTIONS

"The criminal law consists principally of five punishments, which are directed against three thousand offenses," states the Confucian *Book of Filial Piety* (written in about 400 BCE, author unknown). Of these "three thousand offenses," disobedience to one's parents was considered the worst of all crimes. Punishments were imposed for even minor offenses during the Shang dynasty (circa 2000 BCE), according to Zhengyuan Fu, author of *Autocratic Tradition and Chinese Politics*, and were considered extremely harsh even by the ancients. Under Shang law, an offense as minor as littering ashes on a public road was punish-

This image by nineteenth-century British photographer William Saunders shows three Chinese women serving punishment for minor crimes. Other cultures, inclluding those of the West, had similar punishments at the time.

able by the amputation of a hand. The sadistic last emperor of the Shang dynasty, Di Xin (whose wicked ways cost his family the Mandate of Heaven) invented horrible tortures such as forcing people to walk on burning hot bronze plate and cutting out the hearts of condemned criminals.

THE ZHOU AND THE QIN

The Zhou dynasty, which took over when the Shang dynasty fell, wasn't much better. Under their rule, crimes were punished by face tattooing, castration, and nose and foot amputation, in addition to execution. The *Zuo zhuan* historical text provides evidence that the Zhou dynasty cut off plenty of feet, noting: "in the state markets, shoes were cheap but false feet were expensive."

The law of the Qin dynasty, around 200 BCE, was even harsher. Rather than merely executing a criminal for an offense, the Qin would kill three whole branches of his family along with him—parents, grandparents, siblings, and children. The Qin code regulated nearly every aspect of life, right down to the way people farmed food on their own land and included more than seventy forms of punishments: "fourteen forms of execution, sixteen forms of corporal punishments, twenty-seven forms of forced labor, six forms of confinement, and eight forms of property fine."

FOURTEEN FORMS OF EXECUTION

The fourteen forms of execution were particularly gruesome. Some condemned were beaten to death; others were boiled in water or buried alive. Still more were killed by being cut in half or pulled apart by carts, or had holes drilled in their heads or their ribs pulled out. Unsurprisingly, Chinese scholars believe the overwhelming harshness of its legal practices was the major

This illustration from the mid-eighteenth century shows an executioner preparing to beat a prisoner with a bamboo cane.

cause of the Qin dynasty's fall. The law did not undergo significant reform until the time of the Sui dynasty, according to Fu, around six hundred years into the Common Era. Under the Sui code, executions were carried out by the relatively humane processes of strangulation and decapitation, and amputation and mutilation were swapped out for exile, forced labor, and regulated beatings.

DEATH BY A THOUSAND CUTS

This relative humanity toward prisoners didn't last, though. Following a period of political chaos, the Song dynasty emerged triumphant around 1000 CE and implemented the practice of *lingchi*—"lingering death"—to punish severe crimes. As Fu writes, "Execution by slicing is probably one of the cruelest forms of physical torture and capital punishment ever invented. People undergoing this punishment were literally sliced and dismembered in a gradual process until death." Lingchi was adopted by subsequent dynasties and was practiced for nearly another thousand years after its codification into law.

"ALL THE HORRIBLE OPERATION"

T. T. Meadows, a British translator and interpreter, wrote of witnessing the public execution of a band of criminals and their leader in 1851. Thirty-three of the prisoners were executed by beheading, where the executioner would, by flinging his whole body weight into a sitting position as he struck the killing blow, lop their heads off in a single strike. "I think he cut off thirty-three heads in somewhat less than three minutes," Meadows recounted, noting that some of the faces continued to twitch and make expressions for minutes after the separation of the heads from the bodies. Then the same executioner proceeded to cut up the bandits' leader, who was secured to a cross for the process. From Meadows and his companions' position, they could not clearly view "all the horrible operation," as he put it but documented that the slicing went on for about four or five minutes before the body was removed from the cross and decapitated.

Meadows was surprised to see a local man matter-of-factly begin collecting blood from the dead bodies to sell or use for medical purposes and noted that a nearby mother and young

A nineteenth-century print shows a group of pirates awaiting execution in Koolong Bay at Hong Kong.

child "stared hard, not at a sight so common as pigs feeding among human bodies on human blood," but at Meadows and his friends, "the strangely-dressed foreigners." As soon as the door of the execution ground opened, Meadows and his cohorts "hastened to escape from a sight which few will choose to witness a second time without a weighty special cause," he wrote.

Why did ancient Chinese rulers employ such horrible forms of punishment, and why did they remain in use for so much of its history? According to Zhengyuan Fu, these traditions are the result of China's size and the nature of its governance, in which total and absolute power rested in the hands of the emperor. Laws were designed to protect and enforce the power of

SMALL MERCIES

Lingchi was always horrible but sometimes not quite so cruelly inflicted as it was in the case that Meadows witnessed. Its nickname "death by a thousand cuts" is exaggerated, according to many accounts, and it was not unusual for families and friends of the condemned to bribe the executioner to kill the victim immediately before performing the requisite cutting and dismemberment, thereby reducing the condemned man's suffering. In other cases, the victim was killed first and the cutting of the body was done only after death as an act of humiliation. Death by slicing was finally abolished in the year 1905, when the Chinese penal code was revised.

the emperor, with no consideration for the rights of the individual citizen. Many emperors abused their power to rid themselves of political enemies and defiant family members under charges of treason and disobedience. This penal-focused system of law was cruel and unjust and allowed for the perpetration of atrocities on individuals in the name of the divine power of the emperor until said emperor abused his power too much and lost the Mandate of Heaven in favor of a new dictator. There is no justification for such cruelty when it comes to human rights, but the draconian laws and terrible punishments employed by ancient Chinese emperors were effective in one respect: by keeping the people of their country disempowered and afraid, the ruling dynasties were able to maintain control over an extremely vast population and area of land for thousands of years when long-distance communication was difficult and personal oversight of their subjects was impossible.

GLOSSARY

amputation The removal of a body part.

bêche-de-mer A culinary delicacy made from sea cucumbers.

capital punishment The death penalty.

dai A dark blue-green pigment used for cosmetic purposes in ancient China.

decapitation Beheading.

dynasty A line of hereditary rulers of a country. Periods of Chinese history are often labeled by the dynasty that was ruling at that particular time.

foot binding A painful process by which a small girl's feet would be crushed and tightly wrapped with cloth in order to restrict their size.

golden lotus A euphemism for bound feet.

kaidangku Split-crotch pants worn by Chinese toddlers and babies instead of diapers.

lingchi A gruesome form of execution in which the victim was killed by many slicing cuts.

Mandate of Heaven The idea that the right to rule was divinely granted. A new family would come to power whenever this mandate was lost.

nail guards Decorative protectors worn to shield very long fingernails from damage.

prehistory The period of time before written records came to exist.

silkworm pupae The period in which a silkworm enters an inactive chrysalis form after producing silk in its larval form. Also a popular food in ancient China.

FOR MORE INFORMATION

Asian Art Museum of San Francisco
200 Larkin Street
San Francisco, CA 94102
(415) 581-3500
Website: http://www.asianart.org
The Asian Art Museum of San Francisco owns and displays one
    of the largest collections of Asian art in the world.

Asia Society Museum
725 Park Avenue
New York, NY 10021
(212) 288-6400
Website: http://asiasociety.org/arts/asia-society-museum
The Asia Society is a nonprofit organization dedicated to edu-
    cating visitors and the world's citizens in general about Asia.
    Its New York City headquarters boasts a collection of Asian
    art, including visiting exhibitions.

Calgary Chinese Cultural Centre
197 First Street SW
Calgary, AB T2P 4M4
Canada
(403) 262-5071
Website: http://www.culturalcentre.ca
The Calgary Chinese Cultural Centre is a major Canadian pro-
    moter of Chinese culture, and fosters cultural exchange, holds
    community events, and displays Chinese artifacts.

China Institute in America
125 East 65th Street
New York, NY 10065
(212) 744-8181
Website: http://www.chinainstitute.org
The China Institute in America aims to advance a deeper understanding of China via its programs in education, culture, business, and art.

Chinese Historical Society of America
965 Clay Street
San Francisco, CA 94108
(415) 391-1188
Website: http://www.chsa.org
The Chinese Historical Society of America is the oldest organization in the United States dedicated to preserving the record of the Chinese contribution to America.

WEBSITES

Because of the changing number of Internet links, Rosen Publishing has developed an online list of websites related to the subject of this book. This site is updated regularly. Please use this link to access this list:

http://www.rosenlinks.com/TGH/China

FOR FURTHER READING

Branscombe, Allison. *All About China: Stories, Songs, Crafts and More for Kids*. North Clarendon, VA: Tuttle Publishing, 2014.

Harper, Damian. *Lonely Planet China*. Oakland, CA: Lonely Planet, 2015.

Huo, Christina. *Chinese New Year Picture Book: Spring Festival Facts and Stories for Kids and Adults*. New York, NY: Amazon Digital Services, Inc., 2015.

Jian, Li. *Ming's Adventure with Confucius in Qufu: A Story in English and Chinese*. Shanghai, China: Shanghai Press, 2015.

Keay, John. *China: A History*. New York, NY: Basic Books, 2011.

Li, He, and Michael Knight. *Power and Glory: Court Arts of China's Ming Dynasty*. San Francisco, CA: Asian Art Museum, 2016.

Nunes, Shiho. *Chinese Fables: The Dragon Slayer and Other Timeless Tales of Wisdom*. North Clarendon, VA: Tuttle Publishing, 2013.

Qicheng, Wang. *The Big Book of China*. New York, NY: Amazon Digital Services, Inc., 2015.

Robertson, David. *A Glimpse of China: An Outsider's Inside Look at the Middle Kingdom*. Charleston, SC: CreateSpace Independent Publishing Platform, 2015.

Roche, Jess. *Jaw-Dropping Geography: Fun Learning Facts About the Great Wall of China*. Charleston, SC: CreateSpace Independent Publishing Platform, 2015.

Tse, Brian. *Bowls of Happiness: Treasures from China and the Forbidden City*. New York, NY: China Institute in America, 2015.

Yen Mah, Adeline. *China: Land of Dragons and Emperors*. New York, NY: Ember, 2011.

BIBLIOGRAPHY

Acton, Johnny, Tania Adams, and Matt Packer. *Origin of Everyday Things*. New York, NY: Sterling Publishing Co., Inc., 2006.

Bates, Roy. *10,000 Chinese Numbers*. Beijing, China: China History Press, 2007.

Bossan, Marie-Josèphe. *The Art of the Shoe*. New York, NY: Parkstone Press, 2004.

Carr, K. E. "Ancient Chinese Sewage." History for Kids, June 15, 2015. (http://www.historyforkids.org/learn/china/science/chinasewage.htm).

Chen, Ivan (translator). *The Book of Filial Duty: Translated from the Chinese of the Hsiao Ching*. London, England: Hazell, Watson and Viney, Ld., 1908.

Foreman, Amanda. "Why Footbinding Persisted in China for a Millennium." *Smithsonian*, February 2015. (http://www.smithsonianmag.com/history/why-footbinding-persisted-china-millennium-180953971/).

Fu, Zhengyuan. *Autocratic Tradition and Chinese Politics*. New York, NY: Press Syndicate of the University of Cambridge, 1993.

Garrett, Valery. *Chinese Dress: From the Qing Dynasty to the Present*. North Clarendon, VT: Tuttle Publishing, 2007.

Hoyt, E. P. "Hygiene in Ancient China." *CHEST*, Vol. 61 No. 2, February 1972.

Jackson, Beverly. *Splendid Slippers: A Thousand Years of an Erotic Tradition*. Berkley, CA: Ten Speed Press, 1997.

Lei, Zhang. "The pursuit of beauty." *China Daily European Weekly*, November 16, 2012. (http://europe.chinadaily.com.cn/epaper/2012-11/16/content_15935976.htm).

Levy, Howard. *The Lotus Lovers: The Complete History of the Curious Erotic Tradition of Foot Binding in China*. New York, NY: Prometheus Books, 1991.

Meadows, T. T. "Description of an Execution at Canton." *Journal of the Royal Asiatic Society of Great Britain and Ireland*, Vol. 16, 1856. (http://www.jstor.org/stable/25228672).

Millburn, Naomi. "The Origin of Nail Polish." Synonym.com. (http://classroom.synonym.com/origin-nail-polish-9845.html).

Needham, Joseph. *Science & Civilisation in China, Vol. 7*. Cambridge, England: Cambridge University Press, 2004.

Simoons, Frederick J. *Food in China: A Cultural and Historical Inquiry*. Boca Raton, FL: CRC Press, Inc., 1991.

Stamberg, Susan. "Powerful Portraits Capture China's Empress Dowager." NPR, December, 19 2011. (http://www.npr.org/2011/12/19/143796431/powerful-portraits-capture-chinas-empress-dowager).

Steele, Valerie, and John Major. *China Chic: East Meets West*. New Haven, CT: Yale University Press, 1999.

Wong, Jan. *Red China Blues: My Long March from Mao to Now*. Toronto, Canada: Random House of Canada Limited, 1996.

Zhang, Qizhi. *An Introduction to Chinese History and Culture*. New York, NY: Springer, 2015.

INDEX

ABOUT THE AUTHOR

Jennifer Culp is a medical editor and author of nonfiction science and tech books for children and young adults.

PHOTO CREDITS

Cover, p. 1 Digital Vision/Getty Images; p. 5 dowell/Moment/Getty Images; p. 8 Alex Potemkin/E+/Getty Images; p. 9 Planet Observer/UIG/Getty Images; p. 11 Lindsay Brown/Lonely Planet Images/Getty Images; p. 13 L.F/Shutterstock.com; p. 16 Minneapolis Institute of Arts, MN, USA/Gift of Alan and Dena Naylor in memory of Thomas E. Leary/Bridgeman Images; p. 18 © Natural Visions/Alamy; p. 20 De Agostini Picture Library/Getty Images; p. 23 Keren Su/China Span/Getty Images; p. 24 Cartela/Shutterstock.com; p. 27 Summer Palace, Beijing, China/Bridgeman Images; p. 29 Bridgeman Images; p. 34 Private Collection/Bridgeman Images; p. 36 Kean Collection/Archive Photos/Getty Images; p. 38 Photos 12/Universal Images Group/Getty Images; cover and interior pages Lukiyanova Natalia/frenta/Shutterstock.com (splatters), idea for life/Shutterstock.com, Ensuper/Shutterstock.com, ilolab/Shutterstock.com, Sfio Cracho/Shutterstock.com, Apostrophe/Shutterstock.com (textures and patterns)

Designer: Michael Moy; Editor: Philip Wolny; Photo Researcher: Philip Wolny